A WORD FOR TODAY

Audrey Perdue

A Word for Today

The Word of God is the absolute best way for you to encourage yourself. Reflecting on both the good and bad experiences in your life, will help you to find strength and motivation to move forward to your destiny.

Romans 8:28 says, "And we know that all things work together for good to them that love God, to them who are the called according to his purpose."

Purpose is intentional. You have a prophetic destiny! Your mistakes are to teach you and not condemn you. I want you, my friend, to be Blessed, be Challenged and be Confident, because...

There is a Word for Today!

Psalm 119:104 (NIV)

**I gain understanding from your precepts;
therefore, I hate every wrong path.**

We are living in an age where information is abundant. While this technology is remarkable, it also brings the ideas and thoughts of both famous and infamous individuals from all around the world to the palm of your hand. Everyone seems to be speaking "their truth." Yet, there remains only one true way to understanding, and that is through the Word of God. His laws and precepts are as relevant today as they were over 2,000 years ago. Let God's Word be your directive, or you may find yourself on the wrong path.

What ways can you use technology to share your testimony about the things God has done in your life?

_____

_____

_____

_____

_____

_____

_____

_____

_____

_____

_____

_____

Genesis 18:14 (NIV)

Is anything too hard for the Lord? I will return to you at the appointed time next year, and Sarah will have a son.

I have a question for you: Is there anything too hard for the Lord? You may have a lot going on right now, but I challenge you to call on the name of the Lord and entrust Him with your cares. At the appointed time (I call it due season), He will come to set your captive heart free, heal your wounded soul, break every addiction, and provide for your every need.

Nothing—absolutely nothing—is too hard for God. The clock is ticking; the time is already set in the corridors of heaven. He is on His way... Rejoice!

List some things that you are believing God for!

_____

_____

_____

_____

_____

_____

_____

_____

_____

_____

_____

_____

_____

Philippians 2:3 NIV

Do nothing out of selfish ambition or vain conceit. Rather, in humility, value others above yourselves.

Have you ever said or heard the statement, "How in the world could they do that? I would never do this or that... Just get over it and stop doing this or that?" Take time to address your own weaknesses and shortcomings instead of condemning others. Extend to others the same grace you extend to yourself. Christ shows us so much compassion so that we can be compassionate toward others. Let "selfie" be a picture, not your attitude about yourself.

How can you show someone compassion today?

_____

_____

_____

_____

_____

_____

_____

_____

_____

_____

_____

_____

_____

_____

Luke 1:32 (NLT)

He will be very great and will be called the Son of the Most High. The Lord God will give him the throne of his ancestor David.

I have heard it said, "It's not what you are called, but what you answer to." May God be praised! He has many names, and He answers to them all: Wonderful Counselor, Savior, Immanuel, King of Kings, El Shaddai, Jehovah, Lamb of God, Way Maker, Burden Carrier. These are just a few of His names. What does God call you? When He calls, be sure to answer!

To God, I am:

_____

_____

_____

_____

_____

_____

_____

_____

_____

_____

_____

_____

Ezekiel 2:7 (NIV)

You must speak my words to them, whether they listen or fail to listen, for they are rebellious.

Have you ever seen children playing? If one says something the other doesn't want to hear, they cover their ears and shout, "I can't hear you!" We live in a society that doesn't want to hear what the Word of God says. God's words are just as relevant today as they were in Ezekiel's time. Read and meditate on a scripture you can share with someone who may not know the Lord as the pardoner of their sins. Remember, they cannot hear you if you do not tell them.

What Scripture will you share?

How will you explain the scripture?

_____

_____

_____

_____

_____

_____

_____

_____

_____

_____

_____

Luke 19:42 (NLT)

How I wish today that you of all people would understand the way to peace. But now it is too late, and peace is hidden from your eyes.

Today is a new day, one you have never seen before. Once it is gone, you will never see it again. Do not close your eyes to the beauty of this day. Take a moment to thank God for this day and what it means in your life. Ask Him to renew, refresh, and restore the Word embedded in your heart so that you can have peace today and exemplify His peace wherever you go.

This day I will represent the Lord by......

_____

_____

_____

_____

_____

_____

_____

_____

_____

_____

_____

_____

Judges 2:10 (NLT)

After that whole generation died, another generation grew up who did not acknowledge the Lord or remember the mighty things He had done for Israel.

I can remember Sundays from my childhood. Pastors, community leaders, and family members would gather for dinner after church. They would talk about the goodness of the Lord, the things He had done, and the things He was doing.

Now, years later, many of those people have passed, and family gatherings are rare. But I continue to build on the faith in God that was imparted to me. Put your cell phone down for a few minutes and talk to the young people God has placed in your life. This generation needs to know about the goodness of the Lord. Share how He made ways for you, favored your life, and opened doors for you. They need to hear it.

What are you going to say to someone that needs to hear about the goodness of the Lord?

_____

_____

_____

_____

_____

_____

_____

_____

_____

_____

_____

Galatians 6:2 (NLT)

**Share each other's burdens, and in this way
obey the law of Christ.**

When little children have something and another child is
present, we encourage them to share. The same principle
applies to your life in Christ. Paul reminds us that we don't
have to carry our burdens—be it family problems, financial
struggles, illness, or the general cares of life—all by
ourselves. Ask God to place people in your life whom you
can trust to share your burdens, pray with you and for you,
and provide insight from His Word. We are not alone. Share
each other's burdens, and in doing so, fulfill the law of
Christ.

What is heavy on your heart today?

_____

_____

_____

_____

_____

_____

_____

_____

_____

_____

_____

_____

_____

Psalm 139:16 (NLT)

You saw me before I was born. Every day of my life was recorded in your book.

Every moment was laid out before a single day had passed.

Whenever I return to my hometown, I often meet an elder in the community who will say, "I knew you when your mother was carrying you in her belly." This reminds me that they remember me even before I could remember myself.

You are not a mistake; you are not here by accident. God planned you. He is the One who records your days and holds the plan for your life. Every moment of your life is laid out before your Creator. You may plan your day... but the Lord will order your steps!

Lay your plans for today before the Lord and watch Him
order your steps.

_____

_____

_____

_____

_____

_____

_____

_____

_____

_____

_____

Psalm 119:18 (NIV)

Open my eyes that I may see wonderful things in your law.

It amazes me that when a passage of scripture is read to a group of people, each person can draw something different from it—something that speaks uniquely to their situation. This is the power of the Word of God! His spiritual truth (law) is a wonder to behold.

Ask God to open your heart to His Word.

Ask Him to illuminate your mind so that you may experience the wonder of His Word.

Grab your Bible, read Psalm 119:1–18, and discover the wonderful truths our Savior desires to reveal to you.

This accentuates the power of the Word of God!

Write down how you feel after reading Psalm 119: 1-18.

_____

_____

_____

_____

_____

_____

_____

_____

_____

_____

_____

_____

Genesis 6:8 (KJV)

But Noah found grace in the eyes of the Lord.

Our heart's desire should be to find grace (undeserved favor) in God's eyes. Seeking acceptance through social media, ungodly relationships, or material things will only lead to frustration. Instead, our focus should be on pleasing the Lord.

Take a moment to reflect on your life, your relationships, your habits, and your accomplishments. Will God find grace in you today?

Fill in the blank with your name!

But _____

found grace in the eyes of the Lord.

Write down the things that you feel are occupying
unnecessary space in your heart.

_____

_____

_____

_____

_____

_____

_____

_____

_____

_____

_____

_____

Matthew 14:27 (NKJV)

But immediately Jesus spoke to them, saying, "Be of good cheer! It is I; do not be afraid."

"It is I." Three simple words with profound meaning. When Jesus spoke these words, He declared the fullness of who He is:

I am the Way. I am the Truth. I am the Light.

I am the Beginning and the End.

He is saying, "I am whatever you need me to be in your life." Right now, no need is too great or too small for Him to handle.

Whatever God needs to be in your life this very moment express it:

_____

_____

_____

_____

_____

_____

_____

_____

_____

_____

_____

Job 5:8 (NKJV)

But as for me, I would seek God, and to God I would commit my cause.

Everywhere you turn, there seems to be a new way to find the meaning of life. There are countless relaxation exercises, breathing techniques, gurus on every subject imaginable, pathways to enlightenment, methods for success—the list is endless. But the Bible gives us incredibly wise advice: seek God!

List some ways you plan to seek God today:

_____

_____

_____

_____

_____

_____

_____

_____

_____

_____

_____

_____

Joshua 1:5 (NLT)

No one will be able to stand against you as long as you live. For I will be with you as I was with Moses. I will not fail you or abandon you.

God is willing to advise, lead, guide, protect, defend, and cause you to prosper. Be encouraged today! Think about this. God knows everything about you—your secrets, your indiscretions, the things you share, and the things you keep hidden. He knows all of it, every side of the story, and yet He is still willing to stand with you and never abandon you. Who wouldn't serve a God like that?

What will you thank God for today?

_____

_____

_____

_____

_____

_____

_____

_____

_____

_____

_____

_____

_____

_____

Colossians 2:7 (NLT)

Let your roots grow down into Him, and let your lives be built on Him. Then your faith will grow strong in the truth you were taught, and you will overflow with thankfulness.

When we look at a tree, we see the beauty of its leaves, the shade it provides, and the overall splendor of creation. But that's only half of what's happening. Beneath the soil lies the roots, which often spread as far as the longest branch on the tree.

Likewise, we have a strong root system in Christ that we can tap into every day to remain strong, nourished, and resilient through the seasons of life. The stronger our spiritual roots grow—through reading and meditating on God's Word—the more we will flourish in thankfulness to our all-sustaining God.

Today, thank God for the people in your life who deposit into your spiritual root system.

List people to whom you want to make a Godly deposit:

_____

_____

_____

_____

_____

_____

_____

_____

_____

_____

_____

_____

Luke 18:1 (NIV)

Then Jesus told his disciples a parable to show them that they should always pray and not give up.

Prayer is not just a collection of powerless words floating aimlessly in the air, like feathers lost from a bird. Oh no! Prayer is divine communication with our Heavenly Father, our Creator, and our Redeemer—the immortal, eternal King of Kings and Lord of Lords. He delights in having a private audience with us.

Pray always, and never lose hope.

What is your special prayer request today?

_____

_____

_____

_____

_____

_____

_____

_____

_____

_____

_____

_____

Proverbs 12:18 (NIV)

The words of the reckless pierce like swords, but the tongue of the wise brings healing.

There's an old saying: "Sticks and stones may break my bones, but words will never hurt me." But the Bible teaches something vastly different. Words carry immense power—they can pierce the soul, build up, or tear down. They can lift someone from despair and inspire them to keep living.

Choose words that are edifying and encouraging. As Proverbs 18:21 (CEV) reminds us: "Words can bring death or life! Talk too much, and you will eat everything you say." The tongue is powerful; use it wisely.

What are some words that you would use to encourage yourself and someone else today?

_____

_____

_____

_____

_____

_____

_____

_____

_____

_____

_____

_____

_____

Luke 1:38 (KJV)

And Mary said, Behold the handmaid of the Lord; be it unto me according to thy word. And the angel departed from her.

God has made you promises. You might think you're too old, too young, not smart enough, or not good enough for the Lord to fulfill His promises in you. But believe this: God wants to use you! Take Mary's advice and declare, "Be it unto me, Lord, according to Your word."

What promises has the Lord made to you?

_____

_____

_____

_____

_____

_____

_____

_____

_____

_____

_____

_____

Colossians 3:17 NLT

And whatever you do or say, do it as a representative of the Lord Jesus, giving thanks through him to God the Father.

A famous sports brand's slogan is "Just Do It."

As believers, we should adopt a similar slogan: Open the Bible and "just read it," then do what it says.

Today I will represent the Lord Jesus by...

_____

_____

_____

_____

_____

_____

_____

_____

_____

_____

_____

_____

Isaiah 64:4 (NIV)

Since ancient times no one has heard, no ear has perceived, no eye has seen any God besides you, who acts on behalf of those who wait for him.

There never has been, nor ever will be, an idol or false god capable of upholding or addressing the prayers of the righteous. No one has ever heard, perceived, or seen the incredible things the God of heaven has prepared for those who trust in Him.

Our happiness is found in the resource of God. He has something great in store for you. Stay focused and keep moving forward.

What has God promised you?

_____

_____

_____

_____

_____

_____

_____

_____

_____

_____

_____

_____

Mark 9:24 (KJV)

And straightway the father of the child cried out, and said with tears, Lord, I believe; help thou mine unbelief.

In your heart, you believe the Word of God is true. You've seen God work miracles in the lives of others, but do you have the faith to believe He will perform His Word in your life? Be honest with God and yourself. Release your doubt and watch your faith soar.

What are you believing in God for? Make a list and watch God work for your good and for HIS glory!

_____

_____

_____

_____

_____

_____

_____

_____

_____

_____

_____

_____

_____

Exodus 3:11 (NKJV)

But Moses said to God, "Who am I that I should go to Pharaoh, and that I should bring the children of Israel out of Egypt?"

Sometimes you don't feel equipped or worthy to accept God's call on your life. You sell yourself short.

Is it because of a lack of faith in yourself or a lack of faith in the God who has called you to purpose? When God called you, He already knew your past, your quirks, and your shortcomings.

He knows you, and He wants to use you! God is looking at your future in Him.

What has God called you to do? No matter how big or small it may seem, someone is waiting on you!

_____

_____

_____

_____

_____

_____

_____

_____

_____

_____

_____

_____

_____

Embezzlers, adulterers, hustlers, business people, groupies, liars, aristocrats— people from every background and legacy. Sounds like a New York Times bestseller? It is! The Bible is the bestselling book of all time.

In this book, you'll find there is no one the Word of God can't reach, and no one the Word of God cannot relate to.

Pick up your Bible, and I promise you...

You will see yourself.

Who do you most relate with in the Bible and why?

_____

_____

_____

_____

_____

_____

_____

_____

_____

_____

_____

_____

_____

_____

1 Corinthians 15:10(a) (NLT)

But whatever I am now, it is all because God poured out His special favor on me— and not without results.

Who are you? I'm not asking for your job title, social affiliations, or where you live. I'm asking: Who are you when no one is looking?

What gifts has God placed within you?

You are not a self-made person. The DNA of the Creator of the universe runs through your veins. Who you are and what you have accomplished is only by the grace of God. Your experiences, failures, and promotions all come from Him. Only by His grace can you say, "I am what I am, and His grace to me was not without results." His grace makes you relevant, worthy, and favored.

Who are you?

_____

_____

_____

_____

_____

_____

_____

_____

_____

_____

_____

_____

_____

Job 23:10 (NKJV)

But He knows the way that I take; when He has tested me, I shall come forth as gold.

There's a term used today called "cancelling." According to the Urban Dictionary, it means to dismiss, shun, or isolate someone. What I love about God and His Word is that He will not cancel you.

God knows exactly where you are on this journey called life. He is orchestrating your steps to get you where He needs you to be. He may allow trials to test and refine you, but He will purify your vision so you can follow Him clearly and enjoy the blessings He has prepared for you.

You are not cancelled.

Think about a time when you felt the weight of going against the grain in this cancel culture generation we live in and how you saw the hand of God move on your behalf despite the circumstance.

_____

_____

_____

_____

_____

_____

_____

_____

_____

_____

Psalm 118:23 (KJV)

This is the Lord's doing; it is marvelous in our eyes.

There are moments in life that defy explanation—times when God's hand moves in ways that leave you in awe. The beauty lies in knowing that it is the Lord's doing, not your own.

This brings a peace and joy that surpasses all understanding. Let God be the Lord of your life, and watch as He works in and through you to bring glory to His name and satisfaction to your soul.

Write down some things that have happened in your life that you know only the hand of God could have done.

_____

_____

_____

_____

_____

_____

_____

_____

_____

_____

_____

_____

Esther 1:13 (NIV)

Since it was customary for the king to consult experts in matters of law and justice, he spoke with the wise men who understood the times.

Pray and ask God to give you spiritual discernment—the ability to know right from wrong and to understand with keen perception. We live in a time where the line between worldliness and the sacred is very thin. We need to know the truth and stand firm, unwavering under popular opinions. Read and study God's Word to prepare for the times we are living in.

Your prayer:

_____

_____

_____

_____

_____

_____

_____

_____

_____

_____

_____

_____

Proverbs 12:26 (NKJV)

The righteous should choose his friends carefully, for the way of the wicked leads them astray.

You may have Facebook friends or people you occasionally "unfriend" or swipe left on when it suits you. But what about the kind of friend who knows your deepest, darkest secrets and still treats you the same? Or someone you don't give much time to, but they're always there for you?

I encourage you to befriend Jesus and never unfriend Him.

He'll be the best friend you've ever had.

Talk to Jesus. He is the best friend you could ever have.

_____

_____

_____

_____

_____

_____

_____

_____

_____

_____

_____

_____

_____

John 5:8 (NIV)

Then Jesus said to him, "Get up!

Pick up your mat and walk."

What is paralyzing you today? What is hindering you from receiving what God has for you? The very thing holding you captive could be the thing God uses to set you free—if you listen to His voice. Believe God when He says you can do it. Trust Him when He says you are free. Rise up and move forward in the name of the Lord!

What is holding you back from doing what you know God wants you to do? Find scriptures that you can remember to encourage you to move forward.

_____

_____

_____

_____

_____

_____

_____

_____

_____

_____

_____

_____

_____

1 Thessalonians 5:2 (NIV)

For you know very well that the day of the Lord will come like a thief in the night.

I've never heard of a thief scheduling a date and time to rob someone. That's why we set up alarm systems, to at least alert us when something is happening.

Likewise, we should live each day knowing that our King could come at any time. Keep your heart filled with God's Word and your mind ready to follow His instruction—because He's coming like a thief in the night.

How can you prepare for our coming King?

_____

_____

_____

_____

_____

_____

_____

_____

_____

_____

_____

_____

Let's Pray

Father, thank You so much for sending Your Son as the ultimate sacrifice. You loved me so much that You gave Your absolute best for someone like me. May the words of my mouth and the meditation of my heart always be acceptable in Your sight. Keep my heart with all diligence, for out of it flow the issues that hold me captive while I wait for a Word from You.

One Word from You, oh God, can set me free from the things that bind me. One Word from You can straighten the crooked path I walk. One Word from You can make me whole. I submit my circumstances to You and will not look to the right or the left until I receive Your assurance.

Thank You, God! Through You, I can do all things. You have given me the strength to press on. I will seek You while You are near and call upon Your name forevermore. In Jesus' name, I submit my life and all that concerns me to You.

Amen.

Psalm 39:7 (NIV)

But now, Lord, what do I look for?

My hope is in You.

You've tried everything you can think of. You've prayed every prayer, touched and agreed, listened to every sermon, and read all the related books. You've spent your money, time, and resources.

What then gives you the resilience to continue believing and expecting change? The God you serve—that's who. He's come through for you so many times before, and He will do it again.

What are you believing God for today?

_____

_____

_____

_____

_____

_____

_____

_____

_____

_____

_____

_____

_____

Ecclesiastes 10:20 (NLT)

Never make light of the king, even in your thoughts. And don't make fun of the powerful, even in your own bedroom. For a little bird might deliver your message and tell them what you said.

I have voice-activated devices that allow me to "drop in" or send messages to my home even when I'm hundreds of miles away. Long before these technologies existed, Solomon reminded us to be mindful of our words— because someone is always listening.

We serve an omnipotent God who hears everything. The power of life and death is in the words we speak. Choose your words thoughtfully.

Think about a time when you spoke before you thought.
How did that make you feel?

_____

_____

_____

_____

_____

_____

_____

_____

_____

_____

_____

_____

_____

Lamentations 3:41 (NKJV)

Let us lift our hearts and hands to God in heaven.

My little toddler nephew would walk up to me with his hands raised, trusting me to pick him up.

Lifting our hands is a sign of surrender. Lamentations 3:41 tells us to lift our hearts with our hands. Surrender your heart—its desires, affections, and expectations—to God, our Creator and High Priest, who is ready to accept us with open arms. Say this with me: "God, I surrender!"

Reflect on what you are giving away when you surrender.

_____

_____

_____

_____

_____

_____

_____

_____

_____

_____

_____

_____

Matthew 10:30 (NLT)

And the very hairs on your head are all numbered.

I was combing my hair, and there were several strands left in the comb. Did you know that God knows the exact number of each strand that falls out?

If God cares so much about your strands of hair, imagine how much He cares about every intricate detail of your life. A small matter to you is an important thing to God.

List some things that you take for granted every day and then thank God for them.

_____

_____

_____

_____

_____

_____

_____

_____

_____

_____

_____

_____

Romans 12:10 (KJV)

Be kindly affectioned one to another with brotherly love, in honor giving preference to one another.

There's an app for everything these days, including a "kindness app" with ideas on how to be kind to others. Long before apps, the Bible instructed us to be kind.

This verse tells us to be tenderly affectionate and prefer others over ourselves. Respect and consideration for others may seem like a lost art, but it's what we are called to do.

How can you show kindness today?

_____

_____

_____

_____

_____

_____

_____

_____

_____

_____

_____

_____

James 2:18 (NIV)

But someone will say, "You have faith; I have deeds." Show me your faith without deeds, and I will show you my faith by my deeds.

There's a TV show where contestants showcase their talents.

The judges often say, "Show us what you're made of."

Sometimes, faith asks the same of us. Trials and temptations challenge us to reveal the strength of our faith. We show that the greater One lives within us, enabling us to persevere and overcome whatever the enemy throws our way. Have faith to believe and act.

What do you have faith to believe?

_____

_____

_____

_____

_____

_____

_____

_____

_____

_____

_____

_____

Psalm 118:9 (GNT)

It is better to trust in the Lord than to depend on human leaders.

Dignitaries and esteemed leaders may come and go, bringing promises and solutions, but they are only human. As kingdom believers, our trust should be in someone far greater—the One who oversees the universe, rights all wrongs, and died for us before we knew Him.

Who is this? It is Jesus, the Son of God.

How many times have you put your trust in someone and became disappointed?

_____

_____

_____

_____

How did you resolve how you felt?

_____

_____

_____

_____

What did you learn about yourself from the situation?

_____

_____

_____

_____

1 Kings 10:6 (ISV)

**"Everything I heard about your wisdom and
what you have to say is true!" she gasped.**

When I moved to a new area, I relied on reviews for
restaurants and repair services. Reviews often revealed
strengths and weaknesses: "Good work but never on time"
or "Great food but poor service."

As followers of Christ, our actions and behaviors serve as
"reviews" of our faith. Let your life reflect a good report.

If you were being reviewed as a follower of Christ, would you get a good review?

_____

_____

_____

_____

_____

_____

_____

_____

_____

_____

_____

_____

Acts 10:36 (NIV)

You know the message God sent to the people of Israel, announcing the good news of peace through Jesus Christ, who is Lord of all.

Fake news is everywhere—misinformation meant to deceive.

But today, I want to share the Good News, the gospel of Jesus Christ. This news, when heard and applied, will set you free! Don't seek out fake news. Read and live by the Good News.

Read Romans 1:16 and explain what it means to you.

_____

_____

_____

_____

_____

_____

_____

_____

_____

_____

_____

_____

_____

Isaiah 46:4 (NLT)

**I will be your God throughout your lifetime—
until your hair is white with age. I made you,
and I will care for you. I will carry you along
and save you.**

How does this promise in scripture make you feel?

_____

_____

_____

_____

_____

_____

_____

_____

_____

_____

_____

_____

_____

Psalm 77:11 (KJV)

I will remember the works of the Lord; surely, I will remember your wonders of old.

I recently looked through old pictures of family and friends, remembering special moments.

In the same way, reflecting on what God has done for you gives you strength to face today's challenges. The same God who parted the Red Sea is the One who will give you victory!

Make note of the times when you thought you were not going to make it and God came through right on time!

_____

_____

_____

_____

_____

_____

Make note of how God brought you through.

_____

_____

_____

_____

_____

_____

Psalm 86:5 (NKJV)

**For you, Lord, are good, and ready to forgive,
and abundant in mercy to all who call upon you.**

This verse highlights God's attributes: He is good, ready to forgive, and merciful. There are no restrictions on receiving His blessings—He simply says, "Call me!"

What are you waiting for? Reach out and receive His mercy and grace.

How are God's attributes a blessing to you?

_____

_____

_____

_____

_____

_____

_____

_____

_____

_____

_____

_____

Acts 1:11 (NIV)

"Men of Galilee," they said, "why do you stand here looking into the sky? This same Jesus, who has been taken from you into heaven, will come back in the same way you have seen him go into heaven."

There's an old saying: "A promise is a promise." I heard it as a child, and I believe it now more than ever.

Jesus is coming back! Scripture assures us that the same way He left, He will return. By His own power, in His own time, the Magnificent King will come in glory, with the host of heaven by His side.

Don't just stand there... Get ready!

How are you preparing for our Lord's return?

_____

_____

_____

_____

_____

_____

_____

_____

_____

_____

_____

_____

Psalm 139:14 (NIV)

I praise you because I am fearfully and wonderfully made; your works are wonderful, I know that full well.

What do you see when you look in the mirror? Do you focus on flaws, or do you see the beauty of the Creator reflected in you? People often say, "Beauty is in the eye of the beholder." I agree, especially when you look at yourself through the eyes of your Heavenly Father.

What do you see when you look in the mirror, try looking through God's eyes.

_____

_____

_____

_____

_____

_____

_____

_____

_____

_____

_____

_____

Isaiah 49:16 (KJV)

Behold, I have graven thee upon the palms of my hands; thy walls are continually before me.

I enjoy watching cozy mystery shows, and one of the first things detectives look for when something happens is clues. The first clue? Fingerprints. Even when you can't see the person, their fingerprints leave an undeniable mark, telling the story of what is unseen.

Fingerprints are unique. No two are the same, and each one leaves a distinct impression.

In life, we may not always see God working, but His fingerprints are all over our lives.

- Remember the time you couldn't pay a bill, but when you called, you found a credit on your account? Fingerprint.

- Remember when you received a disturbing medical report, only for the follow-up visit to reveal no issues? Fingerprint.

- Remember the day you took a different route and later found out there was a terrible accident on your usual path? Fingerprint.

God has engraved you on the palms of His hands. You are always before Him, and He will never forget you.

Can you remember a time when you saw God's fingerprints on your life?

_____

_____

_____

_____

_____

_____

_____

_____

_____

_____

_____

_____

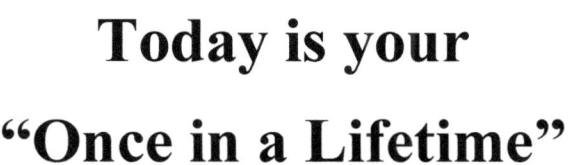

Today is your
"Once in a Lifetime"

Isaiah 40:18 (NLT)

To whom can you compare God? What image can you find to resemble Him?

Anything you can compare to God was made by God. A stunning sunset, a breathtaking mountain view, exquisite blue waters, or pristine white sandy beaches—all of it is God's creation.

God is beyond comparison. He is matchless, sovereign, and independent of His creation. Nothing and no one can compare to the God we serve.

So again, I ask: To whom can you compare God?

No one.

List some of the wonders of the God of all creation and
reflect on the majesty of God.

_____

_____

_____

_____

_____

_____

_____

_____

_____

_____

_____

_____

Matthew 13:55 (NLT)

Then they scoffed, "He's just the carpenter's son, and we know Mary, His mother, and His brothers—James, Joseph, Simon, and Judas."

The people who knew Jesus' family doubted that someone like Him could perform mighty works or possess such great wisdom. They questioned, "Isn't He the carpenter's son?" They recognized His earthly father but didn't know His Heavenly Father. This is the Son of God.

Likewise, remember that you are a child of God. Don't let people define who you are. God and His Word define you.

List some of the positive qualities that God has given you:

_____

_____

_____

_____

_____

_____

_____

_____

_____

_____

_____

_____

We are living in a time when everyone needs encouragement. If you find yourself in need of a lift and there's no one nearby to provide it, don't despair.

There is hope, and it is found in the Word of God.

This devotional workbook is a practical way to inspire you to engage with the Word and encourage yourself.

There is a Word for Today!

I am so grateful to my Lord and Savior Jesus Christ for loving, saving, encouraging, and keeping me.

This book is dedicated to my husband, Elder Nathaniel Perdue. His love, support, and prayers have encouraged me every step of the way. To my sons, Nate IV and Patrick, you are my joy.

I also honor my late mother, father and my aunt, whose wisdom and encouragement to "spend time with God, daily" has been the best gift they ever gave me.

A special thank you to Dr. Toni Lewis, who's like a daughter, your invaluable help and patience made words in a notebook come to life!

I am grateful to bestselling author Traci Wooden-Carlisle who has the God given ability to "understand the words in my heart." I can never thank you enough for all you have done for me.

Psalm 20:27

The spirit of man is the lamp of the Lord, searching all the inner depths of his heart.

www.ingramcontent.com/pod-product-compliance
Lightning Source LLC
Chambersburg PA
CBHW051224120626
46547CB00013B/1494